# THE LIGHT IN ME

By L. M. White

**Copyright © 2024**

**All Rights Reserved**

*"To finding that sliver of light*

*in the creative mind, even when it's hiding in the dark."*

# Table of Contents

Into the Grove ................................................................ 8

Mending Hearts ............................................................ 9

Language of a Poet ..................................................... 10

The Passage ................................................................ 11

Influentials ................................................................. 12

On Evening Air ........................................................... 13

The Dance ................................................................... 14

To Which Sustains ..................................................... 15

Lovely is the Tree ...................................................... 16

Time Between ............................................................ 17

I Knew It Was You ..................................................... 18

Messengers ................................................................. 19

Mercy .......................................................................... 20

Humble Heroes .......................................................... 21

So Little While ........................................................... 22

Let it Rain .................................................................. 23

The Gift ...................................................................... 24

Walk Gently ............................................................... 25

| | |
|---|---|
| Old Glory | 26 |
| Where You Are | 27 |
| Autumn's Anguish | 28 |
| Warrior Soul | 29 |
| What He Didn't Say | 30 |
| Little Birds | 32 |
| Drifting Memories | 33 |
| Nature's Ticking Clock | 34 |
| Blinded | 35 |
| The Tyrant and the Traveler | 36 |
| Bless His Heart | 38 |
| A Christmas Wish | 41 |
| The Mishap | 44 |
| You | 46 |
| Crazy Love | 47 |
| Beside the Sea | 48 |
| Souvenir | 49 |
| A Moment With Me | 50 |
| The Hollyhock | 51 |
| Ghost | 52 |

| | |
|---|---|
| Leah | 53 |
| Déjà vu | 54 |
| Time | 55 |
| A Girl Like Me | 56 |
| In Her Heart | 57 |
| In the End | 59 |
| Paying It Forward | 60 |
| Morning Surprise | 61 |
| The Leader | 62 |
| The Corner Store | 63 |
| Again This Year | 64 |
| Wild About Wayne | 65 |
| Imagine | 67 |
| Dear Son | 69 |
| You | 71 |
| The Man in the Caboose | 72 |
| *Behind the cover* | 75 |

# Into the Grove

It has been a while my friend
Much time has slipped away
Since standing in the warmth of you
Or was it yesterday


For time, you see, stands still my friend
Whenever you are near
I simply can't escape it
The longing to be there


You quiet me inside, dear friend
With all your symphony
Your essence seeps into my soul
It sets my spirit free


So, when it's time to go, old friend
My heart will break in two
Waiting to hear you call my name
I'll come running back to you.

# Mending Hearts

Let us make our way 'cross rolling grasslands
Where blanket flowers and aster are in bloom
And skippers flit like dancing 'round the moon
We'll walk together, come now, take my hand


Take me to the prairie where the brooms
Of Indian grass make music in the wind
The meadowlark sings to its tune and then
Rests upon its twisted golden plumes.


Walk me through the meadows and the fields
Among the scattered larkspur on the hills
Late boneset, her shroud of white bestills
If ever my heart broken, now it is healed.

# Language of a Poet

If we wrote like we talk,

and talked like we write,

there would be fewer published authors

and much better conversation.

# The Passage

Unlike emerald waves 'cross Tuscany
rogue are the swells of the unforgiving
Drake. No fertile fields upon the salty
sea, only desolation in its wake
They round the horn and man the stern within
where Atlas and Magellan do collide,
scattered by the western williwaw winds
and swallowed by its fierce and hungry tide.
Into the depths of murky cold abyss,
bow slowly disappearing in the fray
A thousand souls enveloped in the mist
descending to their final resting place.

Where shipwrecks lay like islands deep below,
a lost maritime archipelago.

# Influentials

How homesick I become

for Wordsworth and Robinson

when sitting down to Robert Burns'

Brigs of Ayr.

# On Evening Air

There's nothing like the magic of a night
That offers such a delicate affair
Descending softly like the cabbage white
She drifts upon the midnight winter air
Her ivory felts and milky waves abound
Like woolen shawls against the earth, she lay
In groves where somber sycamores astound
While blanketing November's shades of grey
We close our eyes, and in her drift we perch
Moonlight glistening in her like the sun
To catch the magic falling through the birch
That melts like drops of sugar on our tongues

Behold the mists of alabaster white
Be still and find the peace within her light.

# The Dance

It's time

The leaves begin to fall

Peppering the ground with golden hues

I can feel it coming

And as if the wind has

Puckered his lips to kiss the earth

A breeze sweeps low across the ground

They begin to tiptoe through the grass

And in mere moments

Their autumn waltz is lifted,

Like the feathers of a bird spinning

In the warm sunshine

Touching me inside

Making me smile

Giving me butterflies.

# To Which Sustains

With highest aspirations, we do dream

And live our lives with hope and to aspire

Of strength for times of vast uncertainty

Whereby our faith must hold us through the fire

And to the thing that one day will reveal

Its lovely consequences we will gain

Conviction true and just beneath the veil

It waits to prove its worth amidst the flame

The cost is not, nor loss is there to be

Belief is truly a beautiful thing.

# Lovely is the Tree

The Chickadee does tell of such a story with his song,

a story of affection for a place where he belongs

He sings of admiration and of generosity

He sings a song of gratitude to his friend, the tree

Its branches ever reaching, warm and sure and true

Strong and deep its roots,

weathering rain or skies of blue

Giving with steadfast gallantry

No doubt of such devotion

No doubt it is the tree


The Chickadee does tell of such a story with his song

A story not just his but too of our beloved home

Each kindred branch implies a cherished family

Reaching out a warm embrace so unconditionally

How fortunate we are, and too the Chickadee

So sweet the song of nature

So lovely is the tree

# Time Between

The length of a day

the stretch of a mile

the span of a year, a very long while

Whether hours away

or if heavens apart

may fond memories of loved ones

stir the hurt from your heart

May the spirit of hope

deliver you peace

and may faith in each other

fill the space in between.

# I Knew It Was You

From the very start I knew

Like the smell of rain before it falls

An expected morning dew

I just knew


Deep in my heart I knew

Like that feeling of déjà vu

I had held you in my dreams

So many times

I just knew


It was the sweetest premonition

A soul known just to me

A gift so strong, so true


I knew son, it was you.

# Messengers

Written in our history are beliefs of native kin

that messengers surround us

silent souls that rest within

perhaps on wings of crimson

on their journey

to transcend


We know not where they linger

but sometimes sense them near

warm and loving spirits

that we hold forever dear

felt for only moments, then all at once

they disappear


Their presence is a sign for

all to cherish things of worth

sending us a message of rebirth

on their way to heaven

from this earth.

# Mercy

It is with Christmas spirit that
we tend to forgo misgivings
We let go and allow ourselves
to love in spite of differences
We nurture and give of ourselves in a way like no other
We become the better side of ourselves.

Such a feeling is like coming home…
Home where we feel comfort, where we are contented
It's only by letting go that we can truly love
It's in that same letting go that allows love to come
back to us.

To forgive is to be open-hearted
And to be forgiven is to be welcomed home.
May your heart and home
be filled with Christmas spirit
now and always.

# Humble Heroes

Love

It fills an open heart, crafting those quiet givers

You've seen them,

They are the elderly neighbor who fixes the woman's gate while she's at work.

And the veteran who pays a mother's bill, leaving the restaurant without a word

They are all around us, giving silently

They are not seasonal

They do not vanish when the lights come down

Go behind and aspire to their goodness

Open your heart

Let it in

Love

# So Little While

Here we are, another year behind us
A year so filled with love and joy and pain
Remembering with the deepest of affection
A year that leaves us each forever changed

A year can sometimes seem to last forever
But really, it's a whisper swept in time
Leaving traces of the ones who went before us
Hiding memories for each of us to find

So here we are, another year before us
A year we'll fill with love and joy and pain
Because we understand that in life's story
With sunshine always comes a little rain.

And when each precious day becomes another
We'll be grateful for each moment passing by
Knowing after all that time is fleeting
And we're only here for just a little while.

# Let it Rain

Abundant sun, a tepid rain

An earthen place by faith sustained

Upon which yields a splendor thing

Spread only from one single grain

A harvest grown, a kinship made

They are, you see, one and the same

Brought on by deeds of selfless gain

To come again with season's change

So, love and give and always know

In all things good, a seed is sown.

# The Gift

If ever you have seen a child,

their mind so filled with wonder

You surely know without a doubt

no longer should they ponder

So put them on your knee

and place it gently in their hands

Open up the doors, and they'll begin to understand

That dreams can linger near, upon a shelf, or in a nook

Magic and adventure can be found within a book.

# Walk Gently

Someone once said…

You are who you are today

because of the people you have known.

You do not get where you are alone

but are shaped by those whose

lives have touched you in such a way

that you will never be the same again.

They are the pebbles that form the foundation beneath your feet, both on the road ahead and on the one you leave behind.

Walk gently on your journey,

for the road will someday lead you home.

# **Old Glory**

Hush, my friends, and listen

for the silence of the night brings with it

a gentle clapping through the winter wind

waving proud, a symbol of hope and freedom,

of courage and of strength.


She is to us as he is to Christmas

The noblest of spirits guiding us home

helping us to overcome

bringing us together as one

Look up, and you shall see them

Fill yourself with their glory

and forget not their valor.

# Where You Are

It is your day, and you're not here

Instead, a memory in the mists of my mind

I often feel you there

Keeping watch

Just out of reach

And if I close my eyes, I can almost feel it

You squeezing my hand

And the sound of your voice

Calling from the mist.

# Autumn's Anguish

Each morning, I awake to love's despair
A fallen leaf amid the morning light
While thoughts of you hang in the evening air
Like burning candles in the dark of night
And as your essence creeps within my soul
I yearn to feel your breath upon my face
A passion deep within me yet untold
That longs to know the warmth of your embrace
As I contend to make my heart be still
The passion and the depth of my desire
For you who knows not of my burning will
Which courses through my very veins like fire.

Perhaps one day to you I will endear
I have so loved you for a thousand years.

# Warrior Soul

No soul returns untouched
To its home, its resting place
It does not tiptoe quietly
Without a sound or trace

Although we may not hear it
It's shouting joyfully
"I've lived, I've learned, I've loved,
And now I've been set free!"

And so, its earthly journey
Comes softly to an end
But another there awaits
In delight to begin again

On a new divine adventure
The grandest yet untold
A soul content within
Carried on wings of gold

And those who dearly loved him
Saw his strength the whole road home
He will forever be
The truest warrior soul.

# What He Didn't Say

The house sat lovely there beside the tracks
Between which stood the stately poplar trees
The engine's blow heard softly in the distance
Growing closer on the summer breeze


Within the house, there lived a man of splendor
The kind of man not many come to meet
His stature tall and disposition tender
A man whose words were always most discreet


He smelled of sweet tobacco when your face
Pressed to his chest
Prince Albert in his pocket
Pipe resting on his lips


His years had seen a many changing people
The world perhaps a less forgiving place
Yet his faith and love for family was unyielding
Given simply with a silent, steady grace

I still recall excitement in the journey
To the house that sat there, lovely by the tracks
A child whose heart was filled with adoration
And now, with fondest memories looking back

His silent soul forever travels with me
And I'll tell him when we meet again someday
That no words were ever needed
It's what he didn't say.

# Little Birds

They are like tiny sparrows in the snow
Jumping, flitting, moving to and fro
Looking, watching, waiting
Never hesitating
To enchant us with their looks,
their warmth,
their glow.

They are like owls
Ever wiser, more than we
Living, laughing, loving life so free
Teaching, guiding, giving
Always so forgiving of us
When we should listen
much more openly.

They are our children
and our saviors
Our lifelong inspirations
Kiss them, hug them,
give them all they need
Put down this verse
and do it now for me.

# Drifting Memories

Leaves fall

Like days from a calendar

Each taking with it a story

A secret so individual

So irreplaceable.

# Nature's Ticking Clock

You gave us a January filled with hope
And all things new
February came on Cupid's arrow
strong and true
Clinging drops of dew breathe signs
of springtime on the move
While quiet showers softly bring
the daffodils in bloom
The warming sun gives birth to seedlings
waiting patiently
Harvested and shared with others
Oh, so graciously
Summer heat takes hold, and soon
the change begins
November skies now bring with her
a brisk and changing wind
Then suddenly December
Much reflection, warming hearts
A whole new start
Again.

# Blinded

The world may be much brighter

should our eyes no longer see

Colors crafted from the heart and not what we perceive

If black and white were hope and peace,

what once was them, now we

United, we would stand as one, no more you or me


Imagine such a world where a greater love precedes

Given to our neighbors near and far across the sea

This love could move mountains

should our eyes no longer see


Creating such a world is up to us,

not you, not me

It must begin together.

It must begin with we.

# The Tyrant and the Traveler

Who is this upon my back?

Bothering me so

You hover oh so near

Casting shadows down below.


Whose unkindly caw

Is screeching high and low

Are you truly what you say

Or is it just for show


You sit beside your brothers

All stately in a row

Wildly, watching, waiting

While the malice in you grows


You are like a witch's broom

Weaving to and fro

Lurking high among the oaks

Where warm winds swiftly blow

I have done no harm to you
This for sure I know
I am just a passerby
No threat do I bestow

Why do you harass me so
You cruel and callous foe
Leave me be; just go
Begged the Owl to the Crow.

# Bless His Heart

Once upon a morning bright,

my bloodshot eyes hid from the light

Praying for just one more bit of rest

While I snuggled in my covers,

suddenly, there came a rustle

As if someone quickly shuffling, shuffling,

through a cluttered mess

"Who goes there?" I muttered,

praying for that bit of rest

*Only this and nothing less*


"It's me, Mama. You must awaken,

for I have lost my special blanky

and cannot eat my breakfast 'til it's found

So slowly, I climbed from my bed,

the blood came rushing to my head

As I stumbled aimlessly around

*My body aching every pound*

Then I felt a gentle tug and saw him
Kneeling on the rug
His eyes began to overflow with tears
I knelt beside him, kissed his sweet skin
Then I stood and nudged his chin
*"It's ok," I said to him*


"We'll look together," I assured him
"I'm sure we'll find your
long lost friend,"
and then a smile began to cross his face,
For there, behind the bedroom door, all
Scrunched up and on the floor
Was his blanky, soft, and worn…
*Just his blanky, nothing more*

So, then we wandered down the hall and
As we entered the kitchen, I saw
His half-attempted breakfast on the wall
Still dripping down the kitchen door
Cheerios piled on the floor
A tiny glass of juice was standing by
*I said nothing, only sighed*

He looked at me, and I looked at him
And then we both began to grin
Then giggles filled the air, yet
Once again
*Oh, what fun, what fun, just me and him.*

# A Christmas Wish

If you were to ask what I wished for this Christmas,

I'd turn and glance your way

Then, fold my hands and bow my head,

and this is what I'd say,

Dear Lord, can you forgive me

for I've forgotten how to pray

I seldom find the time for prayer in my busy day,

But I thought of you this evening

as I was walking down the street,

When a man came up beside me

with no shoes upon his feet,


His clothes were torn and tattered,

no coat upon his back

As I watched him pull a small black book

from an old brown leather sack,

I didn't say a word

as he reached down and took my hand

And as he spoke these words, I began to understand.

Oh, Miss, I hate to beg,

but could you spare a dime for me?

I have no gift to offer but this old black book to read.

The Lord's come knocking at my door,

I've not much time, you see.

I have to make a call today to find my family.

It's been so long I can't recall

what turned our hearts astray,

but if I'm quick, I might

just have one more chance to say

how much I love and need them,

and how grateful I would be

If they could find it in their hearts

to spend some time with me.

So, Ma'am, I mean no trouble,

and I will not ask again if you could

be so kind to lend a dime to this old man?"


And so, I gathered up some change

and held it out to him,

He took it with a smile and said,

"God bless you, my dear friend."

And in my hands, he placed the book,

the cover worn and tattered

But I could not mistake the words.

It was the holy bible

"Keep it close," he said to me as we began to part.

It is a special book, you see,

I know the words by heart."

And with a solemn glance,

he turned and walked away

And left me standing all alone,

not knowing what to say.


One thing I knew for certain

was my Christmas wish would be

For this dear and gentle stranger

to somehow find his family

And they would welcome him and

care for him before his time is gone

For the love he has to offer is the greatest gift of all.

# The Mishap

'Twas the night before Christmas, and Santa was out
In a blustery storm on the roof of a house
When he slipped on some ice and went tumbling down
Pulling with him the packages straight to the ground

"You alright, boss?" yelled Rudolph,
with deepest concern.
"I'm okay," shouted Santa, then he stood and he turned
To find quite a large rip in the seat of his pants
"Too much breakfast," he moaned,
"all those hotcakes and ham."

Well, with all the commotion on such a cold night
The neighbors began to turn on their lights
In a panic, poor Santa attempted to flee
Then his coat somehow caught on the branch of a tree

And there he stood shivering in trousers alone
His coat hanging high, and his boots full of snow
When out of the haze, a large figure appeared
And as it moved closer, St. Nicolas feared
He might not get back to his sleigh on the roof
So, he sucked in his belly and put up his dukes

Then, all of a sudden, a scarf and a coat
Were thrown through the air by a man in the snow
"Oh, why thank you,"
said Santa, the clothes proudly worn.
"You're welcome," said Frosty, "that's what friends are for."

# You

I wake to troubles deep

And answers miles unseen,

Yet my only fear is living

Not having been loved by you.

# Crazy Love

These sunny, funny, lazy, crazy, cozy thoughts of you

Have got me topsy-turvy

spinning webs of powder blue

That sparkle in the sun, they're so much fun;

what shall I do

If all these crazy, funny, lazy, sunny,

cozy thoughts of you

Disappear, oh how I fear the chance

they never may come true.

# Beside the Sea

If you and I could take back time
Would we forever be
The same two people as today
With worries ten times three

Or would our lives be simple ones
Of fairytale delight
Like tine little children
They rest their heads at night

Or would we wake up each morning
Hearing yesterday's affairs
Roving through our memories
As if bees upon the air

Oh, if we could for just a moment
Still, the maker's tide
I think that we would vow to be
A whisper, not a cry

For today, we know what we did not
In days of auld lang syne
And pleasure in the unadorned
Without a question, why.

# Souvenir

Pictures on my wall

Give faces to each memory

Floating down the hall.

# A Moment With Me

Just a walk with me and you will see

Just a little while alone with me

Just a kiss upon your face and then

In my arms forever, you will be.

# The Hollyhock

A

Pink

Purple

White or

Crimson

Towering

Layer of soft

And flimsy petals

Like the dress of a

Swiftly dancing Cinderella

# Ghost

You are like a house, closed up for the winter

Windows shut, doors locked

Open only is the screen door

To your humble porch

Neglected and desperately needing someone.

I am there, peeking in the window

And wondering if I should go

You do not answer

And I feel helpless

Such a beautiful house


And now I leave down the path away from your door

Stopping only for a moment

for one last sign of you.

# Leah

As suddenly as Summer

Turns to Fall

She appeared

As open as the sky

She let me in

As gentle as the breeze

She touched my heart

She is my new

My sweet

My dearest friend.

# Déjà vu

I've seen you before
Somewhere, sometime

Maybe in my dreams
Or perhaps on the street
Among the others
The strangers

Of course
I could be wrong
I may have recognized you
From my life before

Crazy
No, I'm okay, really
My mind is clear
And cluttered

And, you know
I think I've seen you before
Somewhere, sometime.

# Time

Yesterday was Wednesday

Tomorrow is a new day

And today is mine.

# A Girl Like Me

Upon a stool one day, I sat
With comb and brush in hand
To stroke the locks of golden hair
Bestowed upon my head

When staring back in front of me
With innocence and grace
Was a wondering expression
On a childlike face

Her eyes were green like autumn grass
Her lashes long and swirled
To me, they seemed familiar
Who was this little girl?

Her skin was ivory satin
Her cheeks were a pale pink rose
A stream of tiny freckles
Tiptoe across her nose

As I looked into her eyes, I knew
No doubt was there to be
This was no stranger looking back
But just a girl like me.

# In Her Heart

As my mind begins to wonder

about the days of long ago

I recall a special place that us children loved to go

It was a mansion full of sunshine

where love flowed like a stream

A place of ever-after

where our hearts could wander free


Oh, what a sweet remembrance! I still can clearly see

Us playing hide and seek beneath the willow tree

And rainy days were welcomed with anticipated fun

As we waded through the grassy puddles

barefoot one by one


So enchanting were those windy days

that played a lullaby

Coming from the poplar trees

that seemed to touch the sky

Those summer days and chocolate pies

and pallets on the floor

Dolls we made of hollyhocks,

the sacred cellar door

Oh, what a time of joy it was,

no nothing could compare

To the smell of grandad's breakfast

she so lovingly prepared

Though within that house lives someone else

And our childhood days are gone

There's still a place that's filled with love

A place we all call home

It has no walls or windows and cannot torn apart

The place is ever stronger,

it's within our grandma's heart.

# In the End

I might have wished for riches

I could have wished for fame

Had I thought such things would matter

when the good Lord calls my name

I could have wished for beauty

or possessions all my own

But I'd rather leave the legacy of the giver on my stone

So, I've practiced very hard of late

while all the world's at rest

To close my eyes and hold my hands

intently cross my chest

Giving thanks for all I have and those I hold so dear

Promising to give to others more this coming year

It's knowing that our time on earth is such a little while

That makes the little things in life

so much more worthwhile.

# Paying It Forward

If you could take Today

and wrap it with a bow

Then give it to a stranger

someone you didn't know

Just imagine what they'd say

or consider what they'd do

They might throw in Tomorrow

and give it back to you

How lucky then you'll be

to have two days all wrapped in one

You could look around for Yesterday

to come and join the fun

Then include a bit of Always

and before the evening's end

Forever is the gift you'll have

go give it to a friend.

# Morning Surprise

Early Christmas morn 'bout half past four
Woke the farmer ready for his chores
So out he went the cold, a sudden chill
Toward the barn that sat upon the hill
When passing by the chicken coop
He thought he heard a sound
A grumble, mumble, groan, and then a sigh.

Turning toward the outhouse, he was certain
Through the wind and snow made curtain
What he thought was surely just a misfit calf
Standing as if watching snowflakes pass
So, he trudged the snow in that direction
Then spied a mound upon the ground
A big and red and velvety bundle high.

Now curious and a bit confused
And even just a bit amused
The farmer had to know what was ahead
Then there it was, wearing a sheepish grin
A reindeer staring back at him
Along with giant footprints all about,
"So sorry, sir," said Rudolph.
"I told him to go before we left the house!"

# The Leader

Often saying Thank You

just doesn't seem enough

For all you do and all you give

when things get really tough

And words sometimes just can't express

exactly what I mean

How lucky I feel every day

to work with such a team.


So, set aside the policies

and never mind the rules

Your skills lie in your values,

your ideas are your tools

Be your best, above all else,

be exactly who you are

You're not just an employee,

to me, you are a star.

# The Corner Store

On a little bit of dirt
In a little old town
Stood a little abode
Where the folks hung 'round
With a little extra time
And an old card table
They'd spend a little time
Sittin 'round playing checkers
While a little old man
And a little old woman
Sold candy at the counter
By the old pot-belly oven
And when dusk rolled 'round
And the folks went home for supper
The little old woman
Locked the door and said a prayer
That their little bit of dirt
In the little old town
Would see another old day
Where the folks come 'round.

# Again This Year

It is my month

It is hot and busy

And usually expensive

It is fun and sad

And forever changing my life.

It is August

# Wild About Wayne

There is a young man I know
All of nine years old
In truth he reaches no taller
Than my chin, yet he measures
Up to six-feet-four
As tall as *The Duke* himself.

If you were to skim through
his stack of favorite movies,
you would not find the usual genre
of a grade school boy
but instead would see such titles
as *The Alamo* and *Stagecoach*.

His bed is made of wooden posts,
ornamented with a lasso
and blanketed with a pattern
of cowboys on horseback.

And, on most days he can be found
comfortably in a pair of cowboy boots,
vest, and even a handkerchief
draped around his neck.

In all his uniqueness,
he is truly a cowboy at heart.
*The Duke* (John Wayne) once said,
*"Courage is being scared to death
but saddling up anyway."*

I sometimes wonder
what it will be like
to see that young man as he gets older
and will at some point
lose the cowboy getup.
He will not look the same
on the outside,
but I know on the inside
he will still be saying,
*"Howdy partner."*

# Imagine

…you are still seven years old

and it's that enchanted time of year.

As your mother lovingly nudges

you from your spot beneath the tree,

you turn back for one last glimpse

at the glow of lights

forming a magical mist,

suspended heavenly in the air.

Glittered stockings hang with yawning mouths,

as if caroling to the hearth

from which they hang,

and candles burn sweet apples

from the mantel up high.

Father is perched comfortably,

sipping hot coffee from his chair.

He glances up at you,

twisting his whiskered face to manage a wink

before taking his usual position on one knee.

As you climb aboard his back, wrapping your arms tightly around his neck,

sleep is the furthest thing from your thoughts.

Morning will not come soon enough.

You lie awake listening for the slightest sound that

might confirm your belief in the mysteries

of the holidays, and you fall asleep

wondering…

# Dear Son

I've always known

This day would come

When you would find a girl

To give your heart to

It was hard to imagine

There could ever be

Anyone deserving of it

But I now know she exists

And that you have found her.

You have been a never ending

Light in my life

And I'm glad to share

That light with her

She is likely in another room

Down the hall from you right now

With dreams of making you

A home to be proud of

Journeys you'll take together

And children to hug tightly

You are the sole person

She trusts above all else

So be grateful for her

And always make her feel safe

I have so much love for you

And the man you've become

It is hard to find words to express

How I feel about you

You are everything

Good in this world.

# You

I thought of you today
I'll think of you tomorrow
I'll make a wish for you
Of hope and love and laughter

I'll hug you in my thoughts
My arms wrapped 'round you tight
Rings of gold affection
Like rays of warm sunlight

I'll think of you some more because
My heart just can't surrender
The love I have inside for you
I'll think of you forever.

# The Man in the Caboose

I can still hear it coming

the distant rumble

and can recall the anticipation

as we tried to get to the edge

of the garden before it passed.

Of course, I couldn't go without Granddad

Usually found sitting outside the back door

Beneath the kitchen window

Sometimes napping in his lawn chair

With his baseball cap pulled slightly

Down over his eyes

And always armed with a fly swatter.

I would grab his large hand

And begin to pull him in the direction of the tracks.

He never hesitated or refused my sudden

demand of attention

And as we stood there in the grass

Watching as the powerful locomotive

Made its way toward us

I would place his hands tightly

Over my ears so my hands were free to wave

As the big black engine roared past

There was always a man at the window

His arm resting there

Seeming just as anxious to see us

As we were to see him

And as we stood there

The summer breeze rushing over us

We could see in the distance the last car…

The caboose

And there he was

Smiling and waving to us

As if he was a regular visitor to our supper table

And then it was gone

leaving us as quickly

as it appeared

And as we stood there watching it disappear

We could hear in the distance the

Conductor blowing the horn as he approached town

And I can remember wondering when

He would be making his way

Back to us again.

**Behind the cover...**

*"The day this photograph was taken I was lying on a bench in my father's backyard stretching my legs and taking in the air. It was one of many hard days as we took shifts caring for him through his long journey with cancer. As I lie there looking up, there were many thoughts going through my mind... the crashing together of such a beautiful day with such a sad circumstance... is there really a heaven up there? But just for a moment in the warmth of the sun that seemed to be reaching out and touching me gently, I snapped this random photograph. It is a reminder of the healing power that comes from creativity."*

www.ingramcontent.com/pod-product-compliance
Lightning Source LLC
LaVergne TN
LVHW012035060526
838201LV00061B/4621